Our Baby is Going to Die

By Katrina Villegas
Illustrated by Sandra Herrgott

The road of grief before the death of a sibling. Accepting the loss and understanding what will happen.

A book for children experiencing the loss of a sibling- specifically for families going through termination for medical reasons.

This book is dedicated to my amazing family.

We stick together.
Always and forever.

Joe- *We came out stronger as we always do. I know, you know. Thank you for pushing me to think outside the box with these books. You made the books perfect.*

Caroline- *I hope you read these books and know how strong and courageous you were during this time, and still are now. The way you helped our family through this loss was simply incredible.*

April Rey- *I miss you terribly. With every laugh, and every smile, there is a hint of sadness as I long for you to be here and share in our memories. Wherever you are, my love will find you.*

William- *I am so sorry that you never got to meet April. I'll always believe she had a hand in getting you here safely to our arms. You have two amazing big sisters.*

To EJ and JJ, my precious gifts from God. SH.

This is Caroline.

She's so excited! Her Mama has a baby in her belly. She's really excited to have a baby to play with.

Caroline is also scared and nervous.

She's worried about how the baby might take her toys, and that the baby might cry a lot.

She comes up with a great plan to give the baby a special toy if those things happen.

Caroline is scared, nervous, excited and happy...

all at the same time.

It feels weird to her to have so many
emotions all at once.

Her Mama and Daddy tell her that it's normal and okay to have so
many feelings at the same time.

One day her Mama was talking on the phone.

When she got off of the phone she was crying.

Caroline didn't know what was wrong, but she gave her Mama a big hug and told her everything would be okay.

Later that day, her Mama and Daddy told her that the baby inside of Mama was going to die.

Caroline didn't know exactly what that meant, but she'd had a dog die once. She knew that the dog never came home and that she really missed her.

Her Mama and Daddy told her that the same thing was going to happen with the baby.

The baby wouldn't get to come home and live with them.

The baby was dying and they were all going to have to say goodbye soon.

Caroline's Mama and Daddy told her that they were making a choice to let the baby be born early.

Being born early would mean that the baby would not be in any pain.

They asked if Caroline had any questions.

Caroline had a lot of questions...

"Why is the baby dying?" ----------------------------------

"Did I do something wrong?" -----------------------------

"Why isn't the baby built right?" -------------------------

"What are chromosomes?" ----------------------------------

"Why are we built right and the baby isn't?" -------------

"What happens when someone dies?" ------------------------

"What will happen with the baby's body?" -----------------

"Will I still get to play with the baby?" ----------------

"Am I going to get to meet the baby?" --------------------

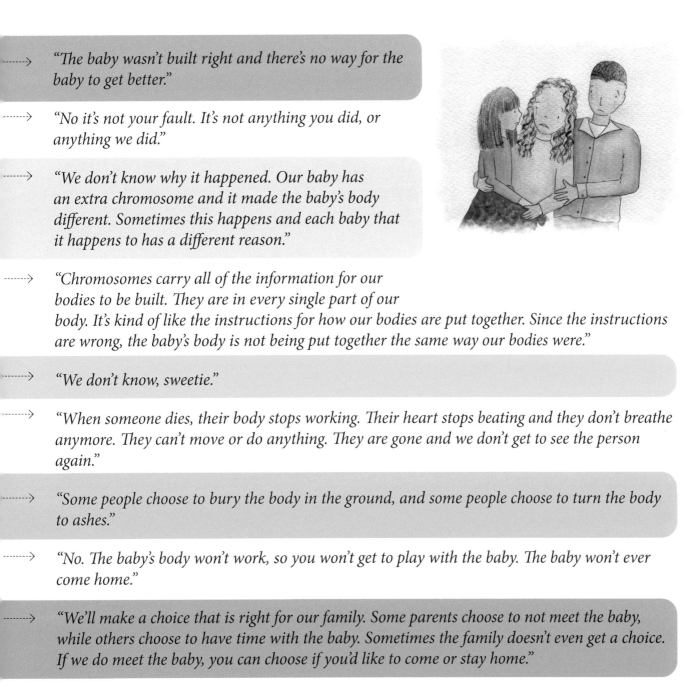

→ "The baby wasn't built right and there's no way for the baby to get better."

→ "No it's not your fault. It's not anything you did, or anything we did."

→ "We don't know why it happened. Our baby has an extra chromosome and it made the baby's body different. Sometimes this happens and each baby that it happens to has a different reason."

→ "Chromosomes carry all of the information for our bodies to be built. They are in every single part of our body. It's kind of like the instructions for how our bodies are put together. Since the instructions are wrong, the baby's body is not being put together the same way our bodies were."

→ "We don't know, sweetie."

→ "When someone dies, their body stops working. Their heart stops beating and they don't breathe anymore. They can't move or do anything. They are gone and we don't get to see the person again."

→ "Some people choose to bury the body in the ground, and some people choose to turn the body to ashes."

→ "No. The baby's body won't work, so you won't get to play with the baby. The baby won't ever come home."

→ "We'll make a choice that is right for our family. Some parents choose to not meet the baby, while others choose to have time with the baby. Sometimes the family doesn't even get a choice. If we do meet the baby, you can choose if you'd like to come or stay home."

15

Caroline had a lot of questions and her Mama and Daddy tried to answer her the best they could.

She asked the questions over and over because the answers didn't always make sense to her.

She asked about where the baby would go after the baby died.

Her Mama and Daddy told her that the baby's energy would always be with them, but that her body would not.

Her Mama and Daddy cried all the time. Caroline was confused and nervous.

Everything was different.

Caroline hadn't cried yet, and she wondered if she should be crying.

She talked to her Mama and Daddy about this and felt so much better. Her Mama and Daddy explained that it was ok to *not* cry. It was also ok if she *did* cry.

All of her feelings were normal and okay.

Caroline really wanted the baby to just come home and for everyone to be happy again.

Her Mama and Daddy told her that they would always keep the baby's memory with them.

Caroline talked with her Mama and Daddy every day.

They talked about what it means to die.

They talked about how everyone was feeling.

They cried and hugged and helped each other.

They talked to the baby as much as they could while the baby was still in Mama's belly.

They also started thinking about ways to remember the baby, and making a plan for the day the baby would die.

-The End-

Our baby's name is April Rey.

She had trisomy 13, which is an extra copy of the 13th chromosome. It caused her body to be built incorrectly.

We chose to let April be born early so she wouldn't feel any pain. April died and never got to come home.

After April died, we eventually had another baby named William. He never got to meet his sister, April.

Caroline is the oldest of her 3 siblings.

We all miss and love April so much. She's not here anymore, but we think about her every day.

A special dedication page for you and your baby.

A special book for _____ , a special big sibling.

(Child's name)

In honor and remembrance of _____ .

(Baby's name)

Draw a picture of how you are feeling:

For Parents:

One of the hardest things about navigating an experience of loss like this, is helping our older children through their grief. When we found out about our baby's diagnosis of trisomy 13, our older daughter, Caroline, was 2.5 years old. We were expecting the news to be hard for her, but we never imagined just how much she'd understand, and how hard it was going to be.

My husband and I learned a lot along the way, and also made some mistakes. As a result, we'd like to share with you what we learned and how to help your child in their grief.

As you read book 1 of this series, it is focused on trying to explain the impending death of a baby to your older child. This is one of the most critical times and also when we learned some of the hard lessons when it comes to children and grief.

Children don't understand the language that adults tend to use. Adults refer to death in many obscure ways. It might feel natural to say things like "passed away," "lost," or "going to sleep," when describing death. Unfortunately, those words are confusing to children.

If you describe your baby dying as "a baby that you lost," your child will take that literally and think that the baby can be found. If you describe your baby as "going to sleep and never waking up," your child might be terrified to go to sleep themselves in fear that they may never wake up.

As a result, we have to be very careful when we speak to children about death. We have to use words that might make us uncomfortable as adults. Death needs to be described in black and white terms. *The baby is dying. The baby is dead. The baby died.*

And death itself needs to be explained as the body failing to work. It is important to tell your child that when someone dies their body stops working, their heart stops beating, and they no longer breathe, eat, walk or talk.

One of the first mistakes we made when talking to our daughter, was telling her in the wrong words. We were emotional and just hadn't thought through things. We told her that the baby was really sick and going to die.

Caroline heard the word sick and thought that it meant sick as in a cold that she might get. She was then worried that she would die if she got sick. We quickly changed our language to say that the baby wasn't sick, but that she actually wasn't built right.

It is so important to just admit to your child when you make a mistake or say something in a way you'd like to fix. We realized immediately that we had used the wrong words. We told her that we'd messed up and then corrected our terminology.

Another thing to remember is that it is ok to not have all of the answers. It is ok to tell your child "I don't know."

This book is kept neutral with regards to any religious beliefs. We took the opportunity to explain some different beliefs about what happens to a person's spirit or energy after death to our daughter, but I've left that up to you so that the book can be used by everyone.

In this book you'll find actual questions that our daughter asked of us at the time. I've tried to recreate our actual discussions with her, along with the appropriate answers that we gave, once we'd found the words to say.

Other key things to keep in mind when dealing with a child's grief:

- Prepare to talk often. Kids need to process. They will ask you the same question over and over and over, day after day, multiple times a day. It is insanely difficult to manage this when in your grief you may not want to discuss it over and over. It is important for children to hear the words several times and in different ways, however.

- Don't hide your own grief. Children need to see that it is ok to cry, be angry, sad, frustrated, mad, etc. Show them your emotions and name them so they know it's ok to have their own. You don't have to continue on as normal without showing emotions during this time. Your child already knows something is wrong, so just let them see you grieve. It is ok and healthy for them. They will show you their emotions freely as a result.

- Don't be afraid to laugh- happiness and sadness can coexist. Children have a hard time understanding that several emotions can be felt at the same time. Adults have a hard time letting it happen when grieving. It is perfectly healthy to laugh and have fun doing something, even while grieving and having intense sad emotions. I've made reference to this in the story so you can start having conversations about this with your child.

- Whenever you can, keep your child's routines as normal as possible. Keep having nap time and play time, keep your child going to school, and doing the activities that you normally do if at all possible. The comfort of the routine is very helpful for children to know that they have stability in their lives.

Our Story

April Rey was diagnosed with trisomy 13 when I was 15 weeks along in the pregnancy. My husband and I chose to induce the pregnancy early to spare her any pain. I was induced at 19.5 weeks. We were able to hold April, make keepsakes, say our goodbyes, and even read her a book. She was alive for 11 minutes, and she was content the entire time. She looked peaceful and knew nothing but love.

I wrote a parenting blog at the time, and I looked to my writing to get me through. It became very therapeutic and I wrote our whole story as it was happening- starting from the very first appointment, and I continue to write about our family and our grief. I've since moved the story over to its own blog that is dedicated to raising awareness about terminations for medical reasons. You can find our whole story and many others at TerminationsRemembered.com.

The Children's Book Series

Did you know this book is part of a whole series on loss? There are 5 books in this series to help walk you and your child(ren) through this experience of grief and loss.

We were SO grateful to have a couple of books about baby loss to read to Caroline when we lost April. It forced us to use the correct language that was otherwise difficult for us. The books that we read helped to really shape our language and make us comfortable talking to our daughter in the appropriate ways. They were the starting point for our wonderful discussions with our daughter and for our growth as parents leading our child through grief.

The books we read were generic baby loss books and could be applied to any type of loss. The two books are "We Were Gonna Have a Baby, but We Had an Angel Instead," by Pat Schwiebert, and "Something Happened," by Cathy Blanford. I highly recommend both.

I really wanted to have a specific children's series for parents walking the path of termination for medical reasons, however. I think there is a unique set of emotions that come with this experience, and I wanted a book to talk directly about it, without talking around the issue.

As a result, I decided to write a children's book series specifically written for parents and children going through the loss of a baby due to termination for medical reasons.

Our Baby is Going to Die.

This book walks you through how to tell your child, *in an effective way*, of the impending loss of their baby sibling. It discusses many of the questions that might be running through your child's mind.

Our Baby Died.

There are 2 versions of this book. One is written for the parents that underwent a surgical termination, and the other is for parents going through termination via labor and delivery.

The books walk your child through what to expect in their grief during these specific moments.

Remembering Our Baby.

This book is for after your baby has died. It walks you and your child through dealing with your grief after the fact, and ways to remember and honor your baby.

The Baby Before You Died.

This book is for your rainbow baby- *the baby born after a loss*. It explains to your child that there was a baby before them that died, and helps them to better understand what happened, while also honoring their potential grief as well.

This book is dedicated to all of the sweet babies loved so fiercely, and lost too soon.

 Please join me in honoring these special babies...

April Rey Villegas	Henry David Joe Gesto	Faith Kinsley Calkins
Ellie-Mae Sarah	Bryson Randolph	Gregory Michael Ewing
Alexander Sage	Lucas Love	Mara Evelyn Dodsworth
Rei Williams	Lily Kroes	Honoré Rota
Clare Briggs	Henry Ryan Whatley	Harry Matthew Jones
William Edward Tucker Hateley	Eddie Alexander Whittier	Lily Winter
Emma Skelton	Millie Rose Sherrieb	Adrian Taylor-Hill
Allegra Joy	Emilia Rose	Jayden Ray Norton
Theodora May Coates	Milo Anthony Cordova	Johnathan Levi
Stella Marie Brash	Jasper Sebastian Zapata	Camila Mae Ramirez
Phoenix Ryder Smith	Pearl Francesca Ashley	Nova Mae Cremer
Laelynn Faith Centric	Angelica Faith Bäume	August Alexander Ainsworth
Gwendolyn Pelletier	Elizabeth Amy Kruse	Georgia Lee
Anka Tuzcu	Nathan Galvan	Levav Arkush Heligman
Christopher Nicolaidis-Romero	Maisie Parker	Riley Allan Dyke
Eila Rose Gray	Emma Paredes-Valdez	Peter John Fletcher
Baby Gray	Margot Faye	Mason James DeJarlais
Harleen Kaur	Oaklee Mae Shipman	Emile Joseph Jubuisson
Asher Wayne Hemesath	Knox Donald Shipman	Jasper Allen Robertson

Callum Michael Wright

Kayden Ruby

Pip McCord

Angel Marsicano Pinter

Alyssandra Riela Foley

Cooper Simpson - Tait

George Michael Rosa

Mars Alexander Robinson

Lyvani F.

Eli Blanco Dennis

Milo Wyatt Bliss

Skye Lee Anderson

Grace Noelle

Jameson Leo

Baby Cade

Willow Smith

Leo Stanfield

D' Antranik Bailey

Ava Rae Ramirez

Laken C.M. Wood

Charlotte Rebecca Lewis

Dahlia Deinlein

DeWayne Deinlein

Rose Deinlein

Ellie Grafton Church

Nicco Cook

Isabelle Violet Harvey

Lily-Anne Styles

Ellie Calder Davis

Dominic Elijah Fisher

Faith Mackenzie Walker

Isaac Wolter Bischoff

Leah Avery Craig

Eliza Persephone Manger

Annabelle Rice Martinez

Arizona O'Quinn

Albert John New

Harvey Peanut Roi

Ava Hope

Jayden Cheng

Valentina Islas

Alexandra Hope Payne

Gabriel Ledford

Brynnlee Ann Williams

Rosie Towndrow

Riley Riesing

Briggs Easton Nawrocki

Samantha Kristine Johnson

Hans Austin

J Gooss

Reid Michael Wilkins

Grace & Lennie

Jo Sutton

Christopher Dalton

Bastian Philip Meyer

Hunter Tyler Nalezynski

Maggie Sophia Correnti

Aiden Ralston

Eithan Dyer

Baby Klar

Baby Bob Mussett

Kamilah Esther

Bodhi David Coultas

Parker Allen Trietsch

Maeva Monroe Hojsan

Eliana Rose

Isaiah Phillips

George W. Choma

Baby A, B, & C Vargas

Andrew John Garry

Dearest parents,

I am so sorry that you find yourself dealing with such a loss.

Your baby will always be remembered. Know that you are doing a fantastic job of parenting.

There are ups and downs when you are managing a loss like this and the entire family is grieving.

You will make it through. I hope you find these books helpful in your journey.

-Katrina

The remaining pages have been left intentionally blank for coloring and/or notes.

Made in United States
Troutdale, OR
11/18/2024

24968304R00024